Folklore and Legends of the Isle of Wight.

Joanne Thornton

Copyright Joanne Thornton 2011

ISBN: 978-1-4477-9114-0

Acknowledgments

I would like to thank all of my family, for their help in the writing of this book and the research. I would also like to thank the records office, and the Local studies collection for their assistance with research and books.

Contents

Introduction	p6
The Tale of the Druids	p8
Legend of the stone cased well	p21
The Holy Grail	p23
The legend of Lucy Lightfoot	p26
The Pied Piper of Newtown	p30
Molly Downer, the witch of Bembridge	p35
The Duver Church at St Helens	p39
The Legend of Wolverton	p43
The Legend of St Catherine's	p51
The Legend of the Siege at Carisbrooke	p55
The legend of Michael Morey	p58
The Legend of Sir Robert Holmes	p62
Charles I's Rose and rings	p66
The Anglo Saxons on the Wight	p70
The Legend of Godshill church	p75
The Wreck of the Clarendon	p79

The Legend of Puckaster Cove   p81
The Legend of Kings Quay   p86
Bibliography   p90

Introduction

The Isle of Wight is full of many stories from Folklore and Legend. This collection aims to inform and delight the reader with a variety of these tales. Many with a loose basis of truth, some with a basis in factual events that have been glorified over the years. I have aimed to examine any evidence for the tales told within this book.

Much of the Island legends come from the time of the French attacks or from the conversion of the Island to Christianity, along with the Saxon invasions that came with it. These events were highly disturbing for the Island people and understandably have remained in folk memory for many years, changing over time, but still with their basis in the truth.

It must be remembered that many people could not read or write in the past, certainly the vast majority of the population, so all their history and tales were told round the fire side in oral tradition, being retold again and again year after year.

Some of the events mentioned can be seen in written form in the diarist Sir John Oglander's accounts and from the history of the Island written by Worsley. These men were wealthy landowners who had the ability to write down what they saw or had heard from local tradition, thus enabling us to have a written source for some of the Island's history.

Many of the legends have been Victorianised and morals have added to the original stories to make them suitable for the Victorian era and their moralized views of society.

The tale of the Druids

This unusual tale has a lot of myth mixed into it, but could some of it have a factual basis? It starts by telling of the IOW, which was then known as the land of Guitt. This name comes from ancient British and signifies separation. The Island was first colonized by the Cimri, after these peoples came the men of Galedin in boats without sails. The Galedin, it is told came when their land was drowned and the Cimri assigned them land. The two nations lived together in peace and friendship. They tilled the land and only warred against the wolf and the boar. The Druids governed over them, as they knew the history of dark antiquity. The Druids contemplated the stars, and could foretell the future. They communicated their knowledge in dark sayings and symbols so the uninitiated could not access their traditions. They taught the people to worship the Gods and to do no evil, and to exercise fortitude.

A third race came to the land of Guitt, and they were known as the Coranied. They came from the land of pools, thought to be

Holland. These men were said to be giants in stature, and despised other men. They did not come in peace and seized some land for themselves. Thus the Coranied ruled over the land, and the Druids ruled over them. Coll, the Arch Druid presided over the sacred groves and wore a golden chain with the sacred serpents egg. The Greeks and Romans record such an egg, which they say was thought to have been vomited up by serpents and was a powerful talisman, it was supposed to be especially efficacious in legal matters.

The Coranied held three places sacred on the land of Guitt. The first, on the western extremity of the island; where the pale cliffs totter over the ocean and giant rocks rear like towers from the waves. In their midst rising tall and thin from the water stood the sacred stone of Ur. This is thought to be the needles rock which it is said fell in the 18th century.

Old drawing of the original Needles rock.

The second site was on Mottestone hill, where stood the pillar of rock and near it the wonderful Logan stone which swung on its foundation to the summer breeze. Logan stones are common in Britain, Logan being derived from the old English dialect meaning to rock. They are large stones that are so finely balanced that a small force can cause them to rock. They are associated with courts in the past, where the guilt or innocence of the party in question could be determined by the rocking stone. The Logan stone described seems to have become dislodged over the years. Could this be the second stone which lay a few yards to the south of the Longstone before Lord Dillon had it moved a century ago? It is said that Mottes stone comes from 'pleader's stone' or 'speakers stone.' Could this be reference to the fact that a Logan stone did once exist on the spot and this was where trials were held so the pleader could determine their innocence? As can be seen at the end of the tale, the Logan stone is indeed used for this in the ensuing story. It was said that the stone swayed to and fro under the summer breeze, yet the strength of many mighty men could not move it from its place. A child was said to be able to swing it backwards and forwards, but if a man with guilt on his soul tried to move it, the stone would hold as firm as the hill itself. The term Logan comes from the old English 'log', meaning 'to rock.' It was sometimes called 'logg un'. Could the name Long stone actually be a derivation of the the logg un stone? And actually be referring not to the longstone as we know it today but to a stone once located nearby that rocked?

The longstone as it stands today

The third site was the sacred grove of oaks, where once a year, a tall pile of dry wood was built, on top of which it was said they bound a living man, confining him in a vessel of wicker work and sacrificed him with fire.

Brading Haven reclaimed, as it is today.

After a time three strangers arrived on the Island, their wisdom was said to be greater than that of the Druids. It was said that they could read the sprigs of the trees which was the symbols by which the Druids communicated their thoughts to one another. These three men were Christians. The Cimri listened to them, but the Druids of the Cimri held aloof as they feared losing their authority over the people. The Druids of the Cimri sacrificed a white bull at the pillar of Mottestone. The three Christians were there and spoke to the people. The Druids did not like this as the people were listening to them. The Druids summoned the people to the Logan stone. The people all came and one by one touched the Logan stone and it swayed back and forth, but as the three Christians touched the stones it stood firm. The Druids called for the Cimri to stone the Christians as they were not pure of soul, but the Christians shouted that it had not been a fair trial. Then one of the Christians looked behind the stone and saw that the Druids had wedged the rock so it would not move, and showed this to the people. Now those that were friends of the Christians shouted and the Coranied heard the shouting and feared a revolt, so attacked the Cimri and men of Galedin with spears. Some were killed and one of the Christians was missing, but was not among the slain.

Sometime later, the Druids of the Coranied held a sacred mystery on the 6th day of the moon, in the month when the nights are the longest. In the morning, they walked in a long procession to cut mistletoe from the oak, and then returned to the circle of oaks where the sacrifice was to take place. In the sacred grove of oaks where Brading haven is now; All who attended carried chains in their hands. A pale bull was led to an oak which had had its branches cut off. The bull was sacrificed and its blood was sprinkled on the people in attendance. Then the mistletoe was carried around the circle of people. The people then went to their homes apart from the initiated in the sacred mysteries. Two of the Christians stayed behind to join them. They sat on benches within the circle of oaks. The Druids tried the Christian's knowledge with questions. The Christians knew how to read and write according to the mystic form of the Druids and passed the trial. Into the inner circle entered two Druids bearing between them two poles on which rested a wooden chest. They rested the chest on the ground and the youngest opened it. Twelve serpents came forth from it and were lost into the woods. The Arch druid then led them all on a procession into the woods. There were three Druids which they had to pass. They had to give the correct sign to pass, otherwise if they passed while getting it wrong, they were stabbed by a sword. One of the Christians answered wrong and was presented with a hazel rod which is the symbol of rejection, and he could not pass. At the end of the procession was a large vessel of wickerwork, likened to the shape of a ship. An alder tree stood in the midst, like a mast. The wicker vessel as the fire light shone upon it seemed occasionally to move, like it contained a living animal. Before the pile stood a man; a giant in stature. He wore no clothing but his body was painted with red paint. The man identified himself to the Arch druid as Prydwen, the messenger. Three men entered the circle, the first wore a robe of white and carried a vessel of gold, the second wore a robe of black and carried a vessel of iron, and the third was clothed in a grey robe and carried a vessel of brass. Then entered the man painted in red, carrying a sword and a burning torch.

The Arch druid poured the gold vessel's contents onto one of three fires around the dry pile and wicker vessel; it produced flames of red. The contents of the second vessel were poured on the second fire, and it produced black smoke. The third fire produced blue smoke. There was a stone cased well next to the pile of dry wood, this contained sacred water, which the Druids called the water of Annown. The three robed men filled their vessels from the well, and each of them poured water on the fires, they did this three times. Each of the watching men lit a torch from the man in red paint's torch. At this point they seized the two Christians and carried them up to the ladder. They did this because they said the Christians had corrupted the worship of the Cimri. They fastened them into the wicker vessel, which they called Ceridwen. Then the Arch Druid raised his torch and they all lowered their torches together to light the pile.

Just then lightning flashed and thunder rolled, then a rushing was heard and water rose from the well in a column fifty feet high and spread in a deluge all around. Then came a roaring and the sea came rushing in to form a mighty wave; the flaming pile was swept away, along with the men, but the vessel floated and the Christians were saved. The sea never returned to the deep and the hexel ground of the Yar and sacred Gabhanodurum still lies beneath a wide lake. Elder states in his book that when Brading haven was drained by Dutch engineers in the reign of James 1st, a well cased in stone was found in the middle of the harbour. The engineers did in fact drain the harbour, but found that the ground was mainly light sand, the area around the well, was of fertile land. It is said to have cost £7000 back then to reclaim what part of the harbour they managed to drain.

Worsley records this in his history of the Island in 1781. It is not just Worsley who writes about the well being found during the reclamation; Sir John Oglander also mentions it in his account of the reclamation; where he is talking about the various attempts to reclaim the land.

'The last wase made by Sir Hugh Myddleton, and Sir Bevis Thelwell (fyrst a broken cytison, then a Page of ye Kinge's Bedchamber). It wase fyrst begged by one John Gibb, of ye Bedchamber to Kinge James, beinge an olde servant of his fathor's; he sowlde his gyfte to Sir H. Myddleton and Sir Bevis Thelwell; they gave him £1000 for itt. They imployed Dutchmen to winn it, who

putt them to an extraordinarie chardge, at least £2000 besydes ye pourchase. In 1622 they made ye banckes at St. Hellens, and so stoped owt ye seae; and I confesse I wase no bakfrynde to the worke, for it made this part of ye countery both full healthfullor, eased us in our marish walles, and in ye improvement of it olso browght more lande to ye parisch. It wase performed by ignorant Dutchmen that they browght owt of ye Lowe Countery. Although it is now growen a greate haven, insomutch that now a boat of 20 tunnes myght come to ye ende of Wadefylde, where now ye key is, but formerley ye boates came up to ye midle of Bradinge strete; it I am fully perswaded itt wase in Edward ye 3rd tyme only an owtlett for ye fresch, and no salt came in, but then ye ffrench warres beginninge, men neglected wholly this Island, and then ye seae wase upon itt; for **we found after ye inninge of ye haven almost in ye midle therof, a well steined with stones, which argueth it had binn firme lande and inhabited.'**

The Commonplace and Account Book of Sir John Oglander. (OG/90/4)

The Cimri are mentioned in a collection of traditional material known as the triads of the Isle of Prydain, which is the Isle of Britain. It is the middle Welsh term for Britain and in that form is often called ynys prydain; and the Isle of Wight is listed as one of the primary islands of it, alongside Orkney and Man. The Cimri are thought to be the race that was conquered and to mean fellow countrymen or compatriots, and they existed not just on the Island but in other areas of Britain as well. The Galedin are listed as one of the races of Protection that came to the Isle of Prydein; they are thought to be refugees from the lowlands of Holland, and the Coranied were one of the races of violence that came to the Isle of Prydein. There is a suggestion that the Coranied came from Poland or Croatia. Therefore these peoples as mentioned in the legend did have some factual basis.

It is also interesting to note that Brading is the location of early baptisms on the Island, where it is said that the first Christian church on the Island was built.

Legend of how the Stone cased well came into existence

Another legend, included in Stone's book, written in the early 20th century contains a legend which describes how the stone cased well itself was built.

It starts in the time of the Romans, when they were living in the villa at Brading. The tale goes that the master wanted some wine, mixed with water, which was common practice in the past, but the water his servers brought him from the river was bad. One server suggested visiting a hermit, who may help them. The Romans then set out to find the hermit in the Apple Valley and brought him a gift of a golden robe to obtain his help. The hermit agreed to help them and taking up a hazel rod he used divining to find a water source. The hazel pointed to a hidden source below, and they dug down and the water gushed out. They built its sides with wroughten stone and planted trees of oak and ash beside it to provide shade. The tale then tells how the river spirit was angry, and sought revenge on the Romans.

That night it rained and thunder and lightning cracked through the sky, and the river caused a great flood, right up to the villa. The Roman's then panicked and went to the hermit who had found the water for help. The hermit, went to the well, and placed a large stone on it, and sealed it with charm and spell. He declared that woe be to any who should lift the stone from the well and expose the river spirit once more.

The flood then subsided and the ocean retreated, and the hermit, who was a Druid, used his hazel rod to find more clean water for the Romans. Years then passed, and the Roman's had gone back to Rome and the Saxons had invaded the Island. The well, had been long forgotten and the wood around it had grown denser. Later, when the Normans were living on the Island, the tale tells how they found the well while hunting, and drank from it after removing the stone, and so breaking the Druid's spell. The river then came forth again and flooded the haven once more.

The Holy Grail

This poem tells of how Joseph of Arimathea brought the Holy Grail to the Isle of Wight. There is no evidence for the existence of the Holy Grail, yet it has remained the object of many searches over the centuries. The Island is then as good a location as any, though many believe the grail went to Glastonbury and the Chalice well. There was much interest in the romance of the Holy Grail and other similar stories during the Victorian era, and it is likely this is such a story. The tale of the Isle of Wight having the hidden grail goes as follows:

In ancient days of trade in tin,
Was much brave traffic done by sea?
Men sailed in sturdy ships of Oak
Twixt Cornwall, Dorset and the Wight
And sailing thus from Tarsish far
Came Joseph seeking further trade
He who was trusted by our Lord
And kinsman to the blessed maid

From Dorset to the Isle of Wight
Came Joseph with the blessed cup
And gave it to a shepherd true
Who, on the downs, watched clouds and sheep
And when the shepherd heard the tale
Of all the Lord had done for him
He took the cup with reverent care
And hid it in the chalk and stones

Again the world was rocked with wrath
The Devils hate purived the cup
And thus it passed from hand to hand
Of those who lived and died for Christ

The place where lies the wondrous cup
Is hid within those hearts long dead
Though trusted sons learned from their sires
Yet no one dared tell the world
But those who own a simple faith

May yet a glorious visitor see
A magic light will show the cup
Before them glowing in the sky
These shepherds on the downs can see
And fisher folk and others too
The mystic cup, the Holy Grail
Beyond the fields above the sea

The Legend of Lucy Lightfoot

This is not so much the legend of Lucy, but the legend of the medieval effigy that lies in the church. The story of Lucy was a tale made up by the then rector, according to R. Frost. The Rector sold the pamphlets for church funds in the 1960s. There was in fact a Lightfoot family living in the Gatcombe area at the time when the story is set, so presumably the rector obtained his information from the parish records. The pamphlet concludes that the wooden effigy figure that lies in the church was that of Edward Estur, who in 1364 embarked on an adventurous journey with Lucy Lightfoot. However, the story really begins to capture the imagination when it is told that Lucy who lived nearby in the village of Bowcombe began to pay visits to St Olave's church at Gatcombe in 1830. She visits the effigy and sits by him for hours.

The enigmatic Gatcombe effigy

On the morning of 13th June 1831, she visited the church as usual, tethering her horse outside. Whilst she was in the church, a violent storm passed over the island. When the storm was over, a farmer entered the church as he had seen the frightened horse outside, and found it to be empty apart from a shattered dagger once held by the effigy but now lying on the altar. Lucy was never heard of again. It is surmised in the legend that she experienced a time slip and passed into the time of her beloved crusader effigy. Frost, in his research into the legend, discovered that on Appledurcombe hill lies a broken obelisk, which was shattered by lightning in 1831; confirming that there had been a great storm in that year.

The effigy itself and its identity still remain a mystery, there is no evidence to suggest that an Estur did go to the crusades, and the only well known crusader on the Island is Sir Ralph De Gorges, he was also said to have been a Templar. The dog at the effigy's feet according to Professor Mascolinsi is a totemistic animal known as Flacon-Caprice; it is thought to come to life on Midsummer's Eve.

The dog carved at the foot of the effigy

So there you have it, could the family of Ralph de Gorges have hidden the effigy in the church at Gatcombe in order to dissociate themselves from the Templars who were disgraced? Or possibly did the De Gorges give the effigy to the De Insulas of Gatcombe as part of their payment in kind after having wrecked Gatcombe estate on a rampage of violence in 1307? Or was there in fact an Edward Estur?

St Olaves church, Gatcombe

The Pied Piper of Newtown

This legend follows a very similar line to the Pied Piper of Hamelin tale, and was used by the inhabitants of Newtown, then named Francheville to explain their defeat to the French. The town in the 14th century, when this story is set, was a bustling port, and as such had a rat problem. They were eating the grain and all the food, and biting the children. Cats were resorted to but the rats only ate the kittens, so the officials in the town tried poison. This did kill the rats, but the dead bodies spread disease, and many people died as a result. The town decided to offer a reward to the person who could rid them of the rats, and the Pied Piper came along in answer to their pleas. The Pied Piper went to the town officials who told him, he would receive a reward of £500 if he could rid the town of all the rats. This however seems to be an enormous amount of money for that time, perhaps pointing toward the later date of the story.

The piper started to play his pipe, and marched on through the town. He stopped every so often, and the rats came out in their hundreds to follow him down the streets. He passed down Silver Street and Gold Street, and eventually came to the harbour, where he entered a boat. He rowed away, still playing the pipe and the rats followed into the water and drowned.

Silver Street, as it is today. This would have been full of shops and houses at the time the story is set.

Gold Street, as it is today

Newtown Quay, where the Piper supposedly led the rats and the children.

Once all the rats had met their demise, the piper went back to the town officials to collect his reward. The town officials however, seeing just how easily the piper had disposed of the rats were reluctant to now hand over such a large sum, suggesting a much smaller sum. The piper was angry and demanded the larger amount, but the officials refused. The piper left the town swearing his revenge.

As the piper left the town, he started once more to play, and the children of the inhabitants followed him, dancing to his tune, they followed up Silver street and down Gold street, while the town inhabitants waited for the children to return, thinking they would come back after having a dance. The children however never returned. The legend goes on to tell of how the French learned of Franchevilles plight, and when the town inhabitants had grown old and the new children were still infants they attacked the town, knowing no fit fighting men would be there to counter attack. The town was sacked in 1377 by the French and burnt to the ground. Searle suggests that the origin of this tale lies in the Black death, and disease spread by the rats, the island was certainly hit by the black death in the 14th century.

Molly Downer; the witch of Bembridge

The tale of Molly Downer is told in a ballad, how she bewitched the custom men, to get free brandy. She lived as a spinster, in a cottage at Hillway, not far from Bembridge farm. The cottage was thatched and known locally as Witches Hatch. Sources tell how she was the illegitimate child of a Reverend from Niton; Reverend Barwis, and he left her a small annual pittance in his will. Local Bembridge legend tells that Molly came from the wealthy Downer family, who made a lot of money out of smuggling. She must have been a bit of a charmer, and was said to have enticed custom men to her house in order to get free booze. She was attractive, well into middle age, but did not find a suitor. She was of neat appearance, but when she got older, she seems to have been driven into a reclusive state. She must have isolated herself, from the community. She was known as a church goer, to first Brading, then to Bembridge, where she struck up a friendship with the Reverend. She is then said to have turned to witchcraft and stopped attending the church. A woman from the community named Harriet taunted her, and when Molly cursed her, Harriet later was paralysed, so she could not speak and move freely; this was when Molly became feared a s a witch. The local women passing her cottage reported it hung with bottles and dolls with pins. She was also known locally as a healer for minor illnesses; this was even attested to by the local school master who had much faith in her abilities. It is thought she may have suffered from Diogenes syndrome; where the sufferer, lives in squalor, is socially withdrawn and self neglectful. It is likely, she was taunted by the locals for being different and a healer, and did not want to mix with them. It must have become worse when she was thought of as a witch and ostracised even more. The ballad tells how the parson took pity on her and befriended her. She was taken ill, and made a will leaving her house and belongings to the parson. A copy of her will still exists, showing that she did indeed leave all to the Reverend Sir Henry Thompson, who was 3rd baronet of Virkees. Her actual name was Mary Downer, and she was a spinster living in Bembridge. The ballad and an 1844 account of her life do not contain the same information regarding Molly. In particular the 1844 account does not mention the Reverend Thompson which we know must be true due to the evidence of her will.

The 1844 account tells how when Molly died, the villagers ordered her body stripped and searched, as they believed Molly to be in possession of money. Nothing was found however, and she was buried in the local churchyard. No memorial was put on her grave, according to the 1844 account. Yet locally it is said that her gravestone disappeared in the 1960s. The villagers were not very happy at Molly leaving everything to Reverend Sir Thompson, and to counter this he told them that he had burnt her possessions. The house where she lived was sold in the 1880s and rebuilt; it is known as Myrtle cottage today and stands behind the duck pond in Hillway.

Although the ballad, states that after burning her house, to stop any continuing magic, someone took a souvenir and her gravestone mysteriously disappeared. The story of Molly Downer is very similar to other accusations of witchcraft across the country. It is typical that someone outside of the community, a healer, and one who had made 'curses' on others that seemed due to coincidence to have come true.

Furthermore, there is a question of her relationship to the vicar. It was not uncommon for vicars at that time to have sexual relations with members of the community, and even if these encounters were not sexual between the Vicar and Molly, the villagers may have thought their relationship immoral. It is strange how the contempory account has no mention of the Reverend Thompson, yet the ballad speaks of their relationship. Was the contempory account protecting the vicar who was still at the church? A relationship certainly must have existed for Molly to leave all her possessions and house to him, and not to the actual church, as she states that they are for use of himself and his family in the will. Could this really be a tale about village immorality and the community taking action, than one about witchcraft and devilish manifestations?

The Duver church at St Helens

The term Duver is actually an Isle of Wight term for sand dunes, the remains of the St Helen's priory church is situated on the area known as the Duver in St Helens. There are a couple of legends attached to this church, the first being that of the Abbott who was excommunicated for devil worship. The curse goes on to say that the Abbott Aymo, was excommunicated at the beginning of the 14th century. It was rumored locally that the Abbott had sold his soul to the devil, that he performed black rites on the altar, and was master of a bestial coven of witches. The church was said to be cursed and rumour has it that the Abbott continued to preach in the empty church.

Examining the facts of this story however reveals that the church of Brading was given to Breamore priory in compensation for the vexations of Isabella de Fortibus. It was apparently Prior Aymo's excessive activity in this matter that caused him to be publically denounced by the Bishop in 1316. The prior then appealed to Edward II against the prior of Breamore, as the prior of Breamore was declaring that the advowson of Brading church was given to them by Edward I. Therefore it seems that Prior Aymos was involved in an argument and obviously upset an influential lady, which brought about his downfall, and local legend and rumour abounded about witchcraft.

The tower belfry, the only surviving part of the church at St Helen's Priory

The curse tells how the excommunication of the prior led to the downfall of the priory and church, whereas fact tells us that as St Helens was an alien priory, when Britain broke into war with France, all the French monks were removed away from the coasts, as the war took hold, then passed, the priory continued to change hands from French monks to the king and back again. In 1414 all the alien priories were suppressed and given to the crown.

Oglander describes shameful acts being undertaken on the church by foreign sailors. This probably refers to holy stoning, which was undertaken on ships, where heavy stones, usually tombstones were used to sand down the decks.

By the 18th century only the belfry remained of the priory as all the rest had fallen into disrepair. That brings us to the other legend of the St Helens tower. It was decided that the tower would be used as a sea mark by Trinity House, and a team of workmen from Portsmouth were sent over to reinforce the church foundations and brick up the eastern wall. This took place in 1748, as the date is incised into the brickwork undertaken by the workmen. Elder tells how the workmen had to whitewash the tower on the seaward side and set up their ladders against the wall. On climbing up the ladder, they came across a gentleman sat at the top of the tower. By this they were very surprised as they could not see how he got up there. He is described as being in old fashioned clothes. The workmen laughed at the old man, and the old man was cross. He told them that the evening would bring something bad, and told them how the ship of the builders who built the tower had been lost at sea on their way home. The workmen ignored him, and when they turned around to check on him later, found he had vanished. When the men had packed away, they set off back to Portsmouth. The boat never arrived. Apparently, there was no wreckage or any other sign of the boat. The main problem with this story is of course if all the men drowned how do we know that they encountered the old man?

The Legend of Wolverton and the hermit of Culver cliff

The name of Wolverton is said to have come from Wulfhere's town. Wolfhere invaded the Island in 661. The legend of Wolverton is really two rolled into one, as it encompasses the legend of the lost city of Wolverton and the legend of the Hermit of Culver cliff. Now sited in Centurian's copse; a maze of bramble and undergrowth is the location of the medieval village of Wolverton.

This village had a manor and a church, reputed to be dedicated to St Urian. According to legend the village also boasted a holy well, though to which saint this was dedicated remains a mystery. Elder's book on legends refers to a stone cross being above the well, which said the following:

While the oose flows pure and free,

Burg and tune shall happy be,

The net bee heavy in the sea,

And wheaten seed shall yield plenty.

When sained blood in the burn shall well,

It shall light a flame so hot and snell,

Shall fire the burg from lock to fell,

Nor sheeling bide its place to tell,

And Culver's Nass shall ring its knel

This refers to the legend which has built up over the years regarding the fall of the village, and its destruction.

The stream running through the location of the lost village.

Elder tells how the locals recalled that the church was on a neighbouring knoll, as they remembered tombstones and skeletons being dug up there. The story of Wolverton's destruction comes from the recollections of an old local man, which were found on his death.

The story of Wolverton and its downfall begin with the appearance of a merchant in the town. The tale is set in the time of Edward III, the merchant is said to have sold cheap goods to the inhabitants, but disappeared off toward the sea and cliffs at Culver late in the evening. He became a frequent visitor to Wolverton. This man became known as the hermit of Culver and legend says he started to lend money to the inhabitants of Wolverton, and asking for deed to be done as repayment. He tended the sick and told fortunes. The hermit told that if anything bad occurred, then a man in a grey cowl was trying to counteract all the good that the hermit was doing. No one however had seen the man in the grey cowl and started to doubt that he even existed. At length the hermit told the inhabitants of Wolverton that the man in the grey cowl was coming to poison their water supply that came from the holy well. A figure soon did appear at the well, dressed in a grey cowl and carrying a staff. The inhabitants ganged up against him, as they thought he was to poison their well. One man threw a stone that struck the man in the grey cowl on the forehead, and he fell to the ground. The other inhabitants continued to throw stones at the man's body until he appeared to be dead. Blood from the wound on his head trickled into the well. The inhabitants suddenly began to think about what they had actually done, as no one had seen the man do any harm and now he lay dead. The Friar came down from his Church, after hearing the commotion, and shouted 'murder!' 'Who has done this?' 'Will no man speak?' The friar looked at the face covered by the grey cowl and recoiled in shock as he announced to the crowd that the Holy man himself had been murdered! The friar asked again who had murdered the holy man, and a man responded by saying that they had been told that he was an evil sorcerer. The friar replied 'who told you this?' The inhabitants however could not say the name of who had told them as they did not know his name or where he lived. 'Wretched people!' the Friar said. 'You will now bear the well's curse as you have caused the holy man's blood to run in and contaminate the holy water.' The curse said how the town would burn after the holy well was tainted with blood, so the inhabitants all sat around in worried groups thinking about their fate and what they had done. Just then the hermit of Culver came walking down into the town as if nothing untoward had occurred. The inhabitants did not know what to make of the hermits appearance and jolly manner, but one decided to ask the hermit where he lived, and the hermit asked him to join him on his walk home. The inhabitant we are told whose name was Edgar, followed the hermit and arrived at a cave in the cliff.

On arrival at the cave, they proceeded down stone steps going into the cliff, and arrived at a hall. The tale then tells of how Edgar was led into a fantastical world, which can only be described as a kind of Hell. The legend continues saying how a feast was laid on for Edgar and when Edgar stood to say a grace the cavern shook and fell around him. When Edgar woke, he was on the top of the cliff and what had been called Culvers Ness, a rock formation had fallen in the night and crumbled into the sea. The tale continues with Edgar, suddenly spotting lots of ships heading for the Island and on realizing they were French and ships of war, decided to get back to Wolverton very quickly. On arrival at the town Edgar proceeded to tell them of the French fleet and on coming attack in the hope that the town would shut the gates and get ready for an attack, however, as Edgar did not stop at just telling them about the French fleet but proceeded to tell them about his fantastical night inside Culver Ness, the town did not believe him and thought him in a drunken state.

The French however were on their way and not long after people shouted French! French! The gates were closed just in time, but a flurry of flaming arrows flew over the gates into the town. The French then rammed the gate and entered Wolverton. The Lord of Yaverland manor, Theobald Russell came to help, but was killed by the French in the attack. The inhabitants grouped together and charged the French out of the gates, thinking they were winning, until they heard trumpets and horns of the French as some had rowed around into the haven and were entering the town from Wolverton Quay. The inhabitants fled and stood on the hills seeing their town laid to waste and burning. Not long after they heard trumpets coming from Barding down as Sir Theobald Russell, Warden of the Island and Sir John De Langford, constable of the castle came to their rescue. This however did not stop the burning of the town; the church burned with it and none of the inhabitants returned to rebuild their houses. No one ventured to go near the ruins of the cursed town of Wolverton. The tale tells how Edgar's house was spared and stood afterward on Pilgrims Lane.

Many believe that the French may well have burnt Wolverton, as they certainly landed on that side of the Island. The French landed at St Helens in 1340, and this is when Wolverton is said to have been sacked. Theobald Russell was indeed killed in the attack by the French, so these parts of the story are factual. A rental roll exists for the manor of Wolverton in 1398, and a court roll with other manors exists for the 16th century for Wolverton manor which suggests that it was rebuilt to some extent.

Centurian's Copse, where the overgrown city of Wolverton stands today.

The Legend of St Catherine's

It is recorded that just after Easter on 22nd April 1313, a ship named Ship of Blessed Mary was wrecked off Chale. The ship had come from Bayonne. It carried a cargo of 174 barrels of white wine. Many men survived the wreck, but the barrels of wine were removed from the beach. The owners of the ship were from Gascony and being the king's subjects he wished justice to be done. The case was first heard in Southampton on 8th June 1313, and it was told that the barrels had reached the shore on various beaches. The men accused were Walter de Goditon, Richard de Hogheton, John Beysem, and Ralph de Wolverton.

The lawsuit against the prosecuted went from Southampton, to Winchester, then to Westminster and back to Winchester again.

These men did not appear at court even though they were ordered to present themselves. Eventually two attorneys appeared at the court on the men's behalf; stating that the men had not been at Chale on the day in question. The value of the casks was stated as 5 marks, and the total loss to the owners of the ship was decided upon as 1000li. At another hearing it came to light that John Beysem had actually been on Chale beach, Walter de Goditon had purchased 53 casks, Richard de Hogheton had bought 2 casks of wine and Ralph de Wolverton had bought 1 cask. It was finally agreed that Walter was fined 287 ½ marks, Richard 11 marks, John 6 marks and Ralph 5 ½ marks. The goods of the men were retained by the sheriff, to be sold in order to pay their debts, whereas John was kept in custody, probably because he had no goods to sell.

The legend continues that the wine actually belonged to monks in a French monastery, so the king notified the pope who ordered Walter as the chief offender to build a lighthouse up on St Catherine's down to help prevent other ships from being wrecked in the future. It was told that his lavish entertaining on the gentry families was what brought attention to the fact that he had acquired such fine wine in the first place. Therefore this story can be seen as one of morals. It demonstrates how greed can make a man fall foul to the law and to God.

I have not found any evidence of the order for Walter to build the lighthouse, but the evidence of the lighthouse or pepper pot as it is known locally still stands today on the downs. It is thought that there was a hermit there before the lighthouse was built as reference exists to a Walter de Langstrell occupying a hermitage there in 1312. Worsley records that the lighthouse was in place by 1328. A chapel was also built next to the lighthouse for a monk who would tend the light and say masses for the dead. This however came to an end under the reign of Henry VIII and his sequestration of the monasteries.

St Catherine's lighthouse as it stands today on St Catherine's Down.

The Legend of the siege of Carisbrooke

Oglander details that although the French succeeded in sacking Nunwell, Yarmouth and Newtown. They then headed for Newport, where they burnt and destroyed the town, the only surviving building was the church. However, they met their match when they approached Carisbrooke. The castle was under the command of Sir Hugh Tyrell. The French laid siege to the castle in August and September of 1377. Oglander records how the French had heavy losses, due to ambushes by the Islanders, many of the French were hurriedly buried in ditches near to the castle and in what was Nodes Hill. After the shooting of their commander, the French declared they wished to parley. The English bribed them 1000 marks and the French retreated and left the Island.

There are various legends attached to the siege of Carisbrooke, one being that the French were ambushed and slaughtered just north east of the castle, in what used to be Deadman's lane but is today Trafalgar Road.

It is Peter Heynoe that is key to the next legend surrounding the siege. He is recorded by Oglander as having slain the French Commander with his silver bow. It is said he did this through a loop hole in the west section of the wall of the castle. The loop in labelled on the wall, for visitors to the castle. It was said that Heynoe cleverly observed the actions of the commander over several days to establish his routine in order to catch him and kill him with the crossbow.

Some tales tell of how with their commander dead, the French retreated, they certainly asked for a parley and then were bribed according to Oglander, so Heynoe had a great hand in the saving of the Island from further French attack, in that fateful year of 1377.

Peter Heyno, or Peter De Heyno as he was known at the time was Lord of the Manor of Stenbury, between Godshill and Whitwell. He was said to have been able to dent a silver penny at three score ten yards. Heynoes bow is described as being wrought and laid with silver in patterns.

Heynoes loop set in the castle walls above the drum tower.

The Legend of Michael Morey

A lot of myth surrounds the factual story of Michael Morey. The actual documents for the trial at Winchester have been lost, so we can never know the complete story. Kenneth Philips has provided many facts to fill the gaps, alongside the folklore and oral tradition of this murder.

Michael Morey lived at Sullens, which according to Philips was a locality not a dwelling. The deserted house still exists to this day.

As was common in the 18th century, it seems that it was not just Michael's immediate family that lived in the cottage with him, but his extended family as well. The two explanations that folklore have given for the motive of Michael's murder of his grandson are that Michael was after money that his grandson James had been left; the other that James had done something to greatly annoy Michael that day.

One version has it that Michael on realizing just what he had done, burnt the house and the body and ran off to hide in a cave. There he was caught and hung on the downs. This however is pure fiction, as we know that Michael was actually hung in Winchester where he stood trial. Although the trial records themselves have been lost, a contempory account of the trial does exist in the Political state of Great Britain Volume LIV from 1737.

The notes included in this book were probably written by someone who attended the trial or knew someone who did. The account states that James Dove was about 14 when he was murdered, and that his grandfather had brought him up since birth. It states that the child had somehow disobliged Michael, and he pretended they were to go to market, and led James into a wood. Here he murdered him with a billhook. The text then describes the act of the murder, telling how Michael cut off James's head, and mangled the body so as to put it into two wallets he carried with him. This shows how the killing was pre meditated and Michael had intentionally set out that day with murder in mind. It seems by looking at the Rates Book, that Michael was arrested straight away, on suspicion, and his eldest son Richard was charged with looking after him for two weeks. During this time, James's body was searched for. It then seems that Michael disappeared, and a hue and cry was started at Newport to find him. Michael is then recorded as having disappeared for a week, before being found and taken to prison, in order to await trial at the assize courts in Winchester. It was not until October that James's body was actually discovered. The arrest of Michael was due to them having found a blood stained shirt in his house and James's disappearance. As is mandatory for coroners, a jury was called to examine the body and hear the evidence in the woods where it was found, along with the first finder. The body was handed over to the undertakers to be buried at St George's church in Arreton. However the body soon had to be taken up again, perhaps as Philips suggests, to identify the clothing on the body, by Widow Small who may have made James's clothes. The Smalls lived next door to the Moreys in Sullen.

The trial took place on 19th March 1736, because the Julian calendar placed New Year's Day on 25th March. Michael did not plead guilty, or make any representation according to The Political state of Great Britain's account. He was publically hung in Winchester that day. He was to be hung in chains on the Isle of Wight, so presumably his body was transferred to the Island, and then it was hung on a gibbet on what is today known as Michael Morey's hump on Arreton Downs.

The Legend of Sir Robert Holmes

The legend says how a knight of Yarmouth, Sir Robert Holmes was an Admiral in the King's Navy. It is said that he captured New York from the Dutch, and he decided on the name of New York as the Dutch had called it New Amsterdam. A hostile ship came across Sir Holmes's ship as he was out on the ocean, he captured the ship and found a statue onboard, but it had no head! When a sculpture was sent for, to try and determine who the statue was supposed to represent, it was discovered that it was a likeness of the King of France. Sir Holmes commanded the sculpturer to make the head in a likeness of himself.

So the statue which should have been for Royalty became one of Sir Holmes instead.

Sometime later Sir Holmes fell from grace; the legend says he continued to fight the Dutch at sea, even though they were now at peace. He had by the sounds of it turned pirate. For the crime of Piracy he was captured and held in the Tower of London on the command of King Charles II, as to the law, but once it had all blown over, Sir

Holmes was released and King Charles II made him Governor of the Isle of Wight.

Robert Holmes lived in Yarmouth, in what is now the George Hotel. He entertained the King there in 1671, 75 and 77.

He was falsely credited with the capture of New Amsterdam although he did in fact spend much of his career at war with the Dutch. He was a Royalist and very good friends with Prince Rupert. He followed him to the continent after the Civil wars. Holmes undertook an expedition to Gambia and built a fort there, it was mainly in Dutch hands at the time. Holmes is also remembered for bringing a baboon back to England and Guinea gold. On the second African expedition, Holmes was charged with exceeding Orders and taking Dutch ships and forts. He was committed to the Tower on two occasions in 1665, but it was not for piracy, but for his success exceeding even the most unreasonable expectations.

He was released and pardoned and in 1666 knighted and given captaincy of a new ship. He launched a fireship attack and destroyed 150 Dutch merchant ships. This became known as Holmes's bonfire. He was now in high favour and after the third Dutch war;

the King gave Sir Holmes the Governorship of the Island. However Holmes was again to fall from favour when he presented an address from the Duke of Monmouth. A court martial was prepared but Holmes managed to get an acquittal, and stayed Governor until his death in 1692. The statue does still exist today in St James's Church in Yarmouth, and the head does not fit the body as it should, so this part of the legend is factual.

The George, where Holmes once lived.

The statue of Sir Holmes in St James' Church, Yarmouth.

Charles I's Rose and the legend of the rings

During the Civil war, Charles I came to stay at Newport, as a guest at Carisbrooke castle. He had some Royalist friends on the Island, including Sir John Oglander; and decided to come and stay there with a view to getting over to France. However, the Governor of the castle, Col. Robert Hammond, who was the King's chaplain's nephew, was a Parliamentarian. The King initially came to stay as a guest at Carisbrooke.

Cromwell however, soon ordered his imprisonment there. The King stayed at the castle from 1647 – 1648. He was sent from there to London for his trial. He tried to escape while at the castle, the picture of the window below is from one of the rooms from which Charles tried to escape from.

A legend tells of how on the King's arrival in Newport he was given a Damask Rose. Charles Carlton states that as King Charles rode through Newport, a woman gave him the last Damask rose from her garden and offered the King her prayers.

One version of the ballad, state how it was November when Charles passed through Newport town and the rose was the last to bloom that year. A girl of sixteen had picked it from her mother's garden to give to the dethroned King and to offer her prayers for him. This ballad tells how it was a Damask rose that matched the Damask of the girl's cheeks.

A ballad written by Conrad Ferdinand Meyer tells how a young boy gave Charles the rose.

Another legend set in the castle has Charles I befriending a boy, who was the son of Holles the Gunner at the castle. Charles is said to have often talked with the boy and one day when the boy was playing with a sword, Charles asked him what he was going to do with it? The boy replied that he would use it to defend the King against his enemies. The King was so thrilled with this answer, that he gave the boy a signet ring. This is on display in the Carisbrooke Castle Museum, as can be seen in the picture below

The King also bequeathed a ring to Sir Philip Warwick, his secretary of state on the Island. Sir Philip, used one of King Charles's rings to seal letters for him, used for the treaty of the Isle of Wight in 1648. This treaty was Parliament's last attempt to reach a negotiated settlement with Charles I. Parliament annulled the treaty in December 1648, and prepared for the King's trial.

The Anglo Saxons on the Wight

In the year 530, it is recorded in the Anglo Saxon Chronicles that Cerdic and Cyric took the Isle of Wight. The Island was ruled by the Jutes until 686 AD. Cerdic gave the Island to Whitgar and Stuf in 534. Whitgar is believed to have been buried in what we now know as Carisbrooke castle in 544. The castle was known as Whitgarabyrig.

Archaeological evidence from excavated burial sites on the Island, however date Anglo Saxons on the Island at an earlier date. Three Saxon burials were excavated at Carisbrooke castle, dating from the early 6th century. One grave being of a very important male, which some have believed to be Whitgar.

In 661, Wulfhere raided the Island and brought baptized men to the island. He penetrated his ships at Brading haven and seized the town of Wolverton. It is said that he came to free the inhabitants of the Island from Sebert. However unsurprisingly the Angles were seen as a threat by the Jutes and they attacked Wulfhere and his men. Wulfhere however told them that he did not seek to conquer but to free the Jutes, the

Jutes still came forth with weapons, but upon seeing just how many Angles there were, the Jutes were driven up into the hills. Wulfhere rested at Brading and built a church there, it was consecrated by Eoppa the priest in preparation to baptize the Jutes.

Brading Church as it stands today

Wulfhere continued to pursue Sebert and burned his castle at Carisbrooke to the ground, which was then known as Witgarusberig. Then in battle Sebert was slain and Redwald, continued the battle, but was caught by Wulfhere's men. A maiden threw herself at Wulfhere and asked him to save Redwald, and Wulfhere agreed to spare him, and said he would take no prisoners as he came in peace. The fighting stopped and Redwald became a great friend to Wulfhere and they ruled together, until Wulfhere decided to return to whence he came and handed guardian ship of the Island over to Redwald. Not many seem to have converted to Christianity or at least stayed at it, as in 686 Caedwalla invaded the Island, killing all the natives that were not willing to be converted to Christianity. This suggests that the Island was still mainly Pagan at this time. The King of the Wight was killed and his two sons, escaped to a safe place for Jutes in France. However, they were betrayed and the Princes were baptized and then executed. It is said that the remaining Jutes were taken to Brading haven, baptized and then executed.

The Island then remained Christian, and in 897 suffered attacks from the Vikings. This is thought to have taken place at Brading Haven, a Viking sword pommel has been found in the haven, which would suggest that there were indeed Vikings in the area at some point. Local legend holds that the site of the battle between the Vikings and the Anglo Saxons took place at Bloodstone copse, near to Brading haven. Legend has it that the stream that runs through the copse is red in colour due to all the blood split at the battle. However, the red colour actually comes from algae, that has attached itself to rocks in the stream, giving the water the appearance of being blood red.

The river as it flows today in the reclaimed Brading haven

One version of the legend tells how three ships moored and the Vikings came ashore. The English boats, which had followed the Viking ships up the river also moored and followed the Vikings ashore.

After a terrible fight, the surviving Vikings noticed that their ships were floating on the tide as it had come in and set off out of the river. However, their ships were so badly damaged that they were blown into shore and the Vikings were detained and taken to Winchester. Here they were tried in the King's court and hung.

The Legend of Godshill church

In common with a lot of Island legends the legend of Godshill church has its roots in the conversion of the Islanders to Christianity. There are two versions of the event, one more moralized with good against evil than the other, but both have a similar core to the story.

The villagers of Godshill were mainly pagan, until a holy man arrived in the village and preached to them, telling them of God and leading them away from their pagan ways. He was very successful and the people of Godshill converted to Christianity and decided to build a church in which to worship the Christian God.

They chose a spot, one version of the legend tells how the villagers were split between building on top of the hill or in the valley at the bottom. A man, who was apparently the devil in disguise, told them that to carry all the stone up the hill would be a huge task and they would soon get tired, so it was decided that they would build at the bottom of the hill. They started to mark out the foundations, and gathered stone for the masons.

One version of the tale tells how St Boniface appeared at the village and told them that the hill would be a much better option for the church. The villagers however, did not listen, and continued to gather stone at the bottom for their new church.

On retiring to bed, all the villagers left the stone in piles at the new marked out spot for the church, but on awaking they were shocked to find that all the stone had moved to the top of the hill! This was taken as a sign that God wanted his church on top of the hill and the villagers continued to build the church there. From that time onwards the village retained the name Godshill. The land to the south to this day retains the name Devil's acre, after the area where the Devil tried to get the villagers to build the church, so that it would not be prominent and they may forget to attend.

Old postcard view of Godshill church.

Another version of the legend, states that the land where the church officials decided to build the church was on the land of a man who was a great sinner. This man announced to them that he did not think it a good idea to build the church on the land of a man as sinful as he, but they ignored this and laid out the plans and stone for the foundations. On coming back the next day, they were surprised to find the stone gone and thought the man was playing a trick on them. Another man came walking up to them in an angry manner, demanding to know why they were building the church on his land without him being even consulted? The church officials were very puzzled and followed the man up the hill to where he said they were building the church. Here they found the stone and the laid out foundations as they had left them at the bottom of the hill, but now moved to the top!

The bishop was arriving that day to lay the foundation stone, so the villager moved all the stones back to the original spot. Presently the bishop arrived and laid the stone. That night, two men were left to watch over the site and next morning reported that the stones had moved up the hill by themselves and arranged themselves in the same position as before but now on top of the hill. The bishop was sent for and he held council with other senior church members. It was decided to leave the stones on the hill and the bishop consecrated the new site. The village then became known as Godshill.

The wreck of the Clarendon

The ship, Clarendon was wrecked on 11th October 1836. This well known ship was wrecked off Chale and Blackgang Chine in a storm and gale force winds. She was sailing from the West Indies. Those on board had the dilemma of whether to jump into the raging sea or risk staying aboard the ship. Some jumped into the sea, hoping to be washed ashore. A local man, John Wheeler seeing that some of the men were jumping to the sea, quickly took action and managed to save three of the crew. All the others were drowned and over the coming hours washed up ashore.

It was not just men aboard the ship and the bodies of ladies also washed up. One being the daughter of captain Gourlay of Southsea; she strangely washed up opposite her father's house.

The local people took the timbers from the Clarenden using them in their homes and barns. The old Clarendon pub, which is now the White Mouse Inn at Chale, used timbers from the Clarenden. Many of the bodies that were washed ashore were buried in Chale churchyard.

Following this disaster, it was decided to build the lighthouse at St Catherine's point, to try and warn ships of the treacherous rocks lying off the coast there and to stop ships from sailing to far inshore.

The Legend of Puckaster cove

This legend is an unusual tale about fairies and of Puck being in residence in the cove. It suggests that the name of the cove originates from this tale and from the fairy rings that were once found there. The cove was a wild and uncultivated place where Mr Puck was said to hold his fairy revels. A small light could sometimes be seen by the locals in the cove and this was known as Puck's little star. There was a spot on the rough ground which was smooth and had circular marks which sometimes appeared every so often in the grass. These were locally known as fairy rings. The tale begins with John Kann, a labourer from Whitwell, a village not far from Puckaster cove. Mr Kann was said to have been favoured by the fairies. One day his neighbour declared that he was going to build a house on the smooth area in Puckaster cove, as he wanted to marry and start a family. John Kann declared that this was unwise as this was fairy domain and that it was foolish as children born on fairy land were given gin by the fairies so that they did not grow any taller and were then carried off to fairy land to be servants, with a wizen old fairy left in their place to fool the family.

John's friend did decide to take this advice and built a house elsewhere. He got married later that year and John was invited to the celebrations, and wedding feast. Late that night John decided to leave and as he had no light thought he would follow his friend who had left just before him, so following what he thought was his friend's lantern he set off. Presently, he began to become worried as he did not recognize where he was and thought maybe he was following the wrong light. The moon came out just then and he realized he was on the smooth area of Puckaster cove. He could hear tiny voices singing and on looking down towards his feet he saw several tiny people dancing in a ring. While he stood watching, one came up to him which looked like a child of about 5, the fairies began singing that this was Mr Puck. Mr Puck came up to John and climbed up his front holding onto his buttons; he came up to John's face and shoved some brown powder up John's nose. This made John sneeze and as he did so he shrank down to the fairy's size. The fairy's grabbed hold of John and danced with him in a ring. Just then a fairy shouted a warning that a rat was approaching. The fairies armed themselves with grass sticks and poked at the rat until it retreated.

Following this, which for John was a very scary encounter; the fairies resumed dancing and mushrooms began to appear in the ring, with a puffball growing in the centre. John was asked to sit upon the puff ball, while the other fairies sat on the mushrooms forming a ring around John. He suddenly noticed that 2 butterfly like wings had grown out of his back, and that he could fly up into the air. This he tried, but decided to come back down and sit back on the puffball, as he was afraid of owls or other predators.

The fairies had prepared a feast and John feasted with them, then Mr Puck asked John if he would like some gold? John replied that he would very much like some gold, but at present was too small to be able to carry a large enough amount, that would change his life. Mr Puck sung him a rhyme, telling him how to find some gold., he then ordered the puffball John was sitting on to shrivel up, as it did, it then burst and when

John opened his eyes it was daylight and he was back to his original size and all the fairies were gone. Well, John decided to have a look for the gold that Mr Puck had told him about. He followed the instructions and found a flat stone with a hole in it and started to look at the sand around it, and sure enough there were flecks of gold in with the sand. John now had to discover a way to collect the gold without anyone noticing, as Mr Puck had told him that if anyone else discovered the gold, then it would disappear. John decided to turn fisherman, and to collect shells to sell.

Postcard of Puckaster cove

John came to the beach daily and sifted through the sand, hiding the gold he collected in buckets and covering it with limpet shells. He traveled to London 3 or 4 times a year to sell the gold dust, leaving his neighbours to wonder how he made such a good trade in shells and fish. John decided to marry a local girl named Betty, but she quickly became curious about John's unexplained wealth, and started to enquire to John how he made so much money. John eventually told her, but Betty being a bit of a gossip, decided to tell some of her friends. The next time, John went to the beach to look for his gold, he found several others of the villagers in the spot. These villagers had found some gold, but the supply soon disappeared and John had to make do with the wealth he had already acquired.

The Legend of King's Quay

The legend is set in 1215 Ad, just following the signing of the Magna Carta by King John. The King was unhappy with the conditions of the Magna Carta and he had instructed Hugh de Boves to collect an army on the continent to invade England and King John was afraid of the English barons. It is recorded that King John did in fact visit the Island on two occasions, both locations being Yarmouth. The first occasion being May 1206, when he later sailed to France with an invasion fleet; secondly, in 1214, where he is thought to have lodged at Quay Street.

The legend of king's Quay begins with the inhabitants of Whippingham Creek being very surprised by four vessels sailing down their creek. Even more so were they when the strangers alighted their vessels and proceeded to carry many rich items of clothing and furniture into the inhabitant's homes. Any who protested were enslaved by the strangers. The others fled, one fisherman however took offence and told the chief of the strangers that there were many grander dwellings on the Island for them to stay at than the ones in the creek! The chief told the man to hold his tongue and to tell no one of the strangers, the man however continued to argue and the chief ordered him to be hung as a warning to the others.

Presently a Templar knight appeared at the settlement. Informing the chief, who was really King john that he had searched at the castle for him, and told the King, that De Vernon who was in charge of the castle at that time was suspicious of strangers who had reportedly arrived on the Island. The King sent an envoy to talk to De Vernon and to assure him that it was only the King's friends who were on the Island, but that secrecy was paramount.

Some supplies were sent to the King from the manor of Kerne on the island, which was in Templar hands, but they soon became short and the King ordered his men to go and rummage the cargo ships of merchants.

The King decided to prepare a marauding expedition on some wealthy merchant ships he had heard were off Southampton. The king took the supplies and decided to sail around the Island to get back to the creek, so that they were not pursued. On returning to the creek, word had arrived from Winchester that the army was collected and the King was required in Winchester, so the King set sail the following day.

The estuary of Palmers Brook flows into King's Quay and the area is comprised of salt marsh, sand and marsh, with ancient woodland surrounding it. There is a stone bridge, known as Queen Victoria's bridge, which allows crossing of the causeway.

The manor of Kern, lies just north of Alverstone, and was given to the Templar's by Roger de Aula. It was granted to Winchester College in 1558. It is known as Kern farmhouse today and the house in existence dates from the 16th century, but was probably rebuilt on the site of a former house as the manor was held by the King in 1086.

Bibliography

Brummell, J, *Ballads of the Wight,* Newport 1979

Elder, A, *Tales and Legends of the Isle of Wight,* London 1843.

Evans, J Rev, *The Legend of Lucy Lightfoot,* Gatcombe 1960

Frost, R, *Isle of Wight Mysteries,* Shanklin, 1980

Hockey, SF, *Insula Vecta,* Chichester 1982

Oglander, J Sir, *The Oglander Memoirs,* London 1888

The Commonplace and Account Book of Sir John Oglander. (OG/90/4)

Philips, K, *For Rooks and Ravens,* Newport

Searle, A, *Isle of Wight Folklore,* Dorset 1998

Stone, PG, *The Architectural Antiquities of the Isle of Wight,* London 1891

Stone PG, *Legends and Leys of the Isle of Wight,* London 1912

Turner, E, *Encyclopedia of Isle of Wight Words, Pace-Names, Legends, Books and Authors,* 1900

Waller, Ruth, *Archaeological resource assessment of the Isle of Wight: Early Medieval period.* 2006

Worsley, R Sir, *History of the Isle of Wight,* London 1781

In search of the Green lands of the flood; http://webpages.charter.net/anthropogene/arc_vol2_is12.html

www.ingramcontent.com/pod-product-compliance
Lightning Source LLC
Chambersburg PA
CBHW060407050426
42449CB00009B/1926